Outrunning Fear

Outrunning Fear

ONE WOMAN'S ACCOUNT OF
A CHILDHOOD IN THE SHADOW OF
A BRUTAL UGANDAN WARZONE

CHRISTINE GLORY

StoryTerrace

Text Antoinette Tyrell, on behalf of StoryTerrace

Design StoryTerrace

First print March 2022

StoryTerrace

www.StoryTerrace.com

DEDICATION

This book is dedicated to the unknown voices lost in the Northern Ugandan Warzone.

Dedicated to the overcomers and conquerors and survivors of brutal wars.

Dedicated to those facing a type of fear.

I dedicate this book to my family, friends who have been a source of strength over the years.

As you read, may you find strength and courage in the midst of any fear you are facing today.

You can Outrun Fear.

Christine Glory

CONTENTS

PROLOGUE

The loud hammer of my heartbeat filled my ears, momentarily blocking out the noise of everything else around me. Blood coursed through my veins as I struggled to catch my breath. My body was screaming at me, 'Stop, Christine, stop.' It was my brain that told me I had to keep running. No matter what happened, I had to keep running. My survival instinct had kicked in.

Above me, the night sky sprawled, a seemingly endless blanket of black. The rough grass of the scrubland cut at my bare legs, and I knew I would feel the pain later, but now, I had to keep going. Occasionally out of the corner of my eye, I'd see a flash or hear a snap close by as a bullet pierced the air.

'One foot in front of the other, Christine, run until you can no longer hear gunfire,' I told myself. It was a trick I had learned. To concentrate on putting one foot in front of the other, propelling myself in an onward motion. If I focused on that alone I could almost manage to obliterate thoughts of what might lurk in the grass beneath me. It helped me from being overwhelmed by the other dangers, the dangers that skulked in the wilderness around me. A pride of lions resting from their hunt, a deadly snake curled in the grass.

'One foot in front of the other, Christine.' It was a mantra that stopped me from losing control and falling to my knees in surrender.

I could still hear the gunfire in the distance, somewhere in the darkness behind me. It was fainter now, and no longer had the same intensity that it had when it had awakened me. In a well-rehearsed routine, my mother had pulled me from the floor where I slept. She didn't need to explain, the gunfire told its own story.

Quickly dressing, we fled from our home. We joined the unseen others, a human chain, linked by fear. At first, my hand had been safely encased in the reassuring warmth of my mother's palm. We carried nothing with us. The wave of people grew larger and as my eyes adjusted to the darkness I could see the faces of the others, running beside me. As the ground beneath my feet grew more uneven and the number of people around me swelled, I lost my mother's hand, but experience had taught me that I could not stop to look for her. The gunfire was still too close. To stop could mean death.

I ran on and on, for what seemed like hours. I wanted desperately to call my mother's name but feared raising my voice. Now the rapid thud of my heartbeat had become the only noise, but I still kept running. I had no way to measure the time or to be sure how long it had been since I'd heard the last gunshot. I began to see dark mounds on the ground as those who had run with me, began to stop and take their place on the wild earth. Still, I kept going. Some more time passed, and I cautiously slowed. The mounds became more frequent and still there was no gunfire. It was time to stop. As my legs gave way underneath me, I collapsed to the ground. Wrapping my arms around my body I commenced my wait. I had survived.

1

My entry into the world was a traumatic one. The turbulence of an ongoing civil war, waged by rebels against the Ugandan government was the backdrop against which I was born on the 6th of September 1987. My birth took place in my parent's house in a village in the Apac region now known as Oyam District Minakulu Adit Village. At around 2am, my mother started experiencing labour pains. She could not be taken to a health facility because of the distance. I was born at home. My grandmother delivered me, helped by two of my aunts. It was she who cut the umbilical cord and placed me in my mother's arms.

Protection of the new-born baby is of the upmost importance and the custom in my village is that babies are not brought outside the house for eight days after they are born. In addition, the number of people who are allowed to visit the house during those days is limited to very close family members, in a bid to ensure no harm of any kind comes to the child.

Perhaps it was a sign of what lay ahead for me that I was not gifted those precious eight days of safety and nurturing in the warm embrace of my mother and our home. Just two days after my birth, cattle raiders raided my village causing my parents to flee with me. Staying or trying to hide were not options. The Karamojong cattle raiders were notorious for their practice of cannibalism and left devastation in their wake, burning entire villages and killing anyone who got in their way.

My mother recalled to me in later years, seeing the smoke billowing from nearby houses and knowing she had to leave. With the help of my father, she forced herself from where she lay, her first attempt to walk after the ordeal of childbirth. Swaddling me as warmly and tightly as she could, and placing me in a sling across her chest, she struggled out of our home. She and my father emerged into the dark night and began to run for their lives.

Together they headed for my grandmother's house further north, close to the border with Sudan, a run which took them over two hours to complete. Tired and bereft, my grandmother took us in and there we waited until word reached us that it was safe to return home.

Five days later we left and made the journey back to our village. It was not the first time my parents had been forced to go on the run from cattle raiders or rebels, but it did not make them any more prepared for what faced them on their return home. Devastation greeted them. Our house and the houses of our neighbours had all been burned. Our crops had been burned, stolen and all our livestock was gone.

Not only had the cattle raiders taken the meager material possessions we had, but they'd also taken our home and they had taken our ability to feed ourselves.

I have no memory of any of this but sometimes when I close my eyes, I think I can see the scene that greeted my parents when they got home. I imagine the smouldering remains of our house, I see my mother desperately searching through the scorched embers in an attempt to retrieve anything at all – a cooking pot, a piece of clothing or a mat to sleep on. I think about how my father must have felt as he walked out of the village and to our farm. I can almost feel the panic that must have set in as he surveyed the blackened landscape, his mind shaken into a panic as he contemplated how he would feed his wife and his new-born child.

There was nothing left, nothing to be retrieved. Starting over was not a choice but a necessity and there was simply no time to waste. Either my parents were resilient enough to begin again from scratch, or they would die and so would I. Some help did come in the form of aid from the United Nations, but it was the hard work of my parents that got us back on our feet again.

The disturbing events that surrounded me in those early days of my existence should have been enough to balance the weight of good fortune in my favour for the rest of my life. Alas, that was not to be. Not only did those events have a long-term impact on my health and wellbeing but they were a glimpse of what was to come in my life. A glimpse of the struggles and challenges that lay ahead.

But this is not a sad story. It is a story of the resilience that pumped through my veins, passed down to me from my parents and those that came before them – a resilience that I cultivated into a force that would guide me in the years to come. My infant self called on that resilience the day the cattle raiders came and from that day on, it grew stronger and blossomed into a power that would see me through some of the darkest days ahead.

2

For all of my childhood, the village had no electricity, and it is only now that electricity is becoming available. Because of this, life was governed by the sun and the moon. Work started when the sun came up and outdoor activities ceased once darkness fell. Our house, like all of those in the village, had no water supply. A large part of my day, from the age of five, centred on fetching water from the well. The well was located a thirty-minute walk from my home, and I would have to make the journey up to three times a day. When I started making this journey, I was only expected to carry a small amount of water due to my small size but as I grew up, I carried more and more, balancing large water jugs on my head as I made my way from the well to my home. I was always accompanied by other females – my mother or my sisters, aunts and cousins and often other women from the neighbouring houses.

The other activities I helped my mother with were cooking and collecting firewood. We often walked for miles, for three or four hours, to find the firewood necessary to keep us warm and for cooking our food on. There were forests near us which housed dangerous animals, poisonous snakes and other predators. For that reason, we never went into the forest alone.

Farming was the other activity that was core to all our lives, whether you were a man, woman or child. The primary crops harvested on the farms were beans, rice and nuts. I had to learn as a child how to do the hard manual labour of farming – digging, planting and ploughing in order that everyone could eat. Every family had their own land where they would grow the crops to feed themselves. They also had farms where they would grow crops to sell which was the means of paying for school fees and other expenses.

Often, if neighbours weren't successful in growing enough crops, my family and other families would help them out. In times of need, neighbours always helped each other out.

In the culture I grew up in, boys were prized more than girls so there was some disappointment when at my birth, a girl arrived. I was, however, the first born and because of that I was showered with love by everyone in my family – my aunts, my grandmother, cousins and uncles. Not only my family, but the entire community raised me and all the other adults in the village had the right to discipline me, as my parents had the right to discipline our neighbours' children. My siblings and I, along with the other children around us, really were raised by a village. When out in the fields, the women who had recently had babies would carry them in a sling with the baby on their back or chest, allowing them to get on with their work while still taking care of an infant.

Each day would start with the sunrise, usually at around 5.30am. I'd get up with my mother and together we'd get started on the chores. We'd light the fire to boil water and make breakfast. By 6.30, breakfast was eaten, and we'd be out to work on the farm by 7am. After 10am the temperatures became so hot it was impossible to work outside and so, we would return home for the rest of the day, returning to the farm in the evening when the temperatures cooled sufficiently to allow us to work outside again.

When we returned home in the morning, the women would set to work again, preparing for lunch. The men, meanwhile, would sit around at home, listening to the radio and chatting with each other. When lunch was served, we ate what we had grown in the fields, beans and rice combined with the meat from the animals we raised, cattle and goats. At the weekends we would sometimes kill an animal for food, as a treat.

Despite the war that was happening around us and the lack of material things, we felt we never wanted for anything such was the love and security from our family and from our community. We had little in the way of clothes, just a few which were our Sunday best, something to wear to the market and something to wear when working on the farm. When our clothes were ripped, we sewed them and if I outgrew any of my clothes, a seamstress would alter them. Shoes were a luxury, only the rich had shoes and so walking outdoors in my bare feet was second nature to me. Sometimes, sandals were donated to us but that was a real treat. I do recall that there was dust everywhere so perhaps not having lots of clothes was a blessing as it would have meant having to constantly wash them.

There were different levels of poverty within the village. Some of my neighbours were so poor they were unable to buy food, never mind clothes or to come up with the money to get medication for their children if they needed it. Oftentimes, it was in homes where the adults drank a lot of alcohol, that the greatest poverty was felt. For those who were in these situations, other families, including my own, helped them out when they could. My own family established itself as one which offered assistance to others whenever possible, even though we had very little ourselves.

If anyone left the village to go to the nearest city, the capital Kampala, which was over 600kms away, it was assumed that that person must have a lot of money. If anyone had a car, it was a huge deal as so few people had them and they were an incredibly rare sight. Even a bike was a luxury and if you had a motorbike, then you had made it in life. Having a house built from cement was also another sign of wealth and when I was growing up there was only one such family in the entire village.

Although the outside world felt very far away, the events that were happening outside our village had a massive impact on me and my family. I knew from an early age that there was a war going on. One of my earliest memories was of United Nations Workers coming to my village in times of drought, to provide us with aid. I remember queuing up to get the rations of food they would hand out and for me, it was the very first time I saw a white person. As children we were almost more excited about this than we were about getting food and water. We'd rush up to the workers and tried to touch their hair and skin, the colour of which we had never set eyes on before. We watched them all day, fascinated. I am sure they were fascinated by us too and I wondered what type of a world they came from.

I'd watch planes fly in the sky over my village and it did make me think about what else lay out there, beyond what I knew. I couldn't imagine it. It was the only life I knew, and it was the only life my parents had known too. Most people in the village never had the opportunity to leave. Most women stopped attending school once they were finished primary school.

Education was expensive. There was no help from Government after primary school. Private school was the best option but was beyond the means of almost all families. In the Government-run schools there could be up to 150 students in one class. Sometimes, there were no books, and the children would write on the floor in lieu of having paper.

My grandmother had attended school until she was about 12 years old. The primary role of women was to get married and have children and in my grandmother's era, the end of primary school and the start of menstruation was seen as the time when these aims could be pursued. My grandfather was a hunter and did not receive any formal education at all.

My paternal grandfather died when my own father was very young. This left my father, Omara Tony Mambo, from the Otengoro Olang Clan, in a precarious position with the fear that another family member might come along and take his home and land away from him. Securing the family line was of upmost importance so that families would not lose their lands and their livelihoods.

My father inherited a large amount of land, but his neighbour took away a large amount of that. It was a terrible situation that could have escalated into violence, but my father is a peaceful man and let the neighbour have the land. There was more available to him but even so, given the difficulty of making the land sustain a family, it was a heavy blow for him at such an early age.

Issues over land were commonplace, and still were when I was growing up. If the ownership of the land is not made one hundred per cent clear, situations can get out of control and even lead to deaths in some cases with family members and neighbours sometimes going as far as killing each other in order to secure a piece of land.

When such issues arose, the village Chief could be called in to resolve them. A team of elders and the Chief would meet to hear the details of the matter and to make a ruling on what course of action should be taken. Witnesses would be called, and evidence heard until the matter was resolved.

My parents met when my mother came to the market in my father's village. My grandmother used to come there to sell food and my father saw her and wondered who she was. My mother, Atyang Everline, was from Okaro-owok-okwer amor and was just sixteen. My father went to the elders to ask them to approach my mother's family on his behalf. My father needed to get married at the time as he wished to secure the family line, especially given the problems he had already encountered when he inherited the land off his own father.

When they married, my mother moved into my father's family home. My father had a brother, but he was not home very often. He gambled and sold a lot of the family land, putting more pressure on my father to hold on to what land he could. My mother was just seventeen when I was born at which time my father was still a student in secondary school.

Traditional religious practices were still pursued in the village. Traditional herbal rituals were performed, and my grandmother carried out these rituals – a gift which was to work in my favour later on when she stepped in and saved my life when an illness almost killed me. Witchcraft was also practiced, and many people still believed in that although that has now died down.

The mainstream religions practiced were Christianity and Islam. There were Protestant and Catholic churches in the village, which caused a sort of divide between the people depending on which religion they practiced. Neighbours would fall out with each other over differences in religion. On Sunday mornings, all those who followed Protestantism would leave their houses to attend service and then later in the day, the Catholics would head off for mass. My parents took me to a Protestant Church every week and I would attend Sunday school.

While religion divided, there was one thing that did unite the community. It was a gathering of all the men over a drink which would be made in a large pot and shared amongst them all. They'd sit around the pot and drink the alcoholic beverage through long straws in times of celebration such as for weddings. It was something that united them as they sat, laughing and sharing stories about the past.

It was a tight-knit place to grow up despite the differences that sometimes arose but core to it all was the family unit. I was the eldest of eight children, but my next sister was not born until I was three. It gave me a head start and meant as the rest of my siblings arrived, I took on a vast amount of responsibility.

Life in my village was neither luxurious nor particularly comfortable but I was oblivious to this. The love and security provided by my parents and the wider community wrapped me in a blanket of protection of such strength that I never once felt that I was wanting for anything.

Protected I was, but that didn't mean that my parents didn't discipline me. I was beaten frequently but I would take refuge in my grandmother's house. It took two hours to get there on foot which may have explained why I was such a fast runner – I'd speed away when I was in trouble to hide out there. I didn't have to do any work in my grandmother's house, and she lived on the Sudanese border where we could see all sorts of beautiful, wild animals including lions and elephants.

3

When I did need to go to the hospital, my dad would cycle a bike, with my mum sitting on the back, holding on to me. They travelled together, over the harsh landscape, over thirty kilometres to the nearest hospital.

Living in the UK now, and having experienced the health system here, I know it must be difficult for anyone who grew up in a country with accessible public health care to understand the struggle my parents faced in not only bringing me to hospital when I needed to go, but also in getting me seen by medical staff when I did get there. That came down to cold, hard cash. If you had money to pay, you would get medical attention but if you didn't, access to medicine and doctors was denied. For my parents, and the millions of people like them who lived in a world of poverty, this meant devastating choices had to be faced.

The money needed was no small amount and there were times that my parents didn't have what was needed to ensure I was looked after medically. In those times, they would have to sell whatever they could to raise the money –

cattle, crops, anything.

My grandmother practiced traditional herbal rituals and when I was two, she was called upon to intervene when my parents thought I was going to die. It would not be the last time that my parents were convinced that my death was imminent. My grandmother came to our house, my hair was shaved off and she did incisions into my head until blood poured out.

I don't know the exact details of what else she did. I know animals were killed, a chicken and a goat, but before they died, the animals were moved around me in some way, and I was smeared with their blood. This ritual went on for three days after which I came back to life.

During one of my illnesses when I was four, I was suffering from severe stomach cramps. My parents tried desperately to get me into a health facility for treatment but in vain. Eventually, they had to take me to a military detach camp near our home. Medication was administered and thankfully my condition normalized.

Later, I contracted meningitis and this time was hospitalised at Atapara hospital for medication and treatment. Despite receiving treatment, my condition deteriorated so rapidly, that the doctor told my parents there was nothing more that could be done. He advised them to take me home, which really meant, taking me home to die.

There was no hope, and my grave was dug. I remember feeling very cold and shivery. I had severe diarrhoea and could not keep any food down. All my family gathered and prayed together, saying their goodbyes to me. During the night, I awoke suddenly and sneezed and once I sneezed, I asked for food.

In my culture, there is a belief that when someone is about to die, they will sneeze and ask for something to eat. By now, my whole family was in tears believing this to be the moment when they would lose their little girl. The mourning had started. My grandmother and my aunts had travelled to be there and to say goodbye.

Food was brought to me but this time, I managed to keep it down. A few days later, I was still alive, and I asked to be allowed to leave the room where I was. They brought me outside and I lay down in the air, glad to feel a breeze. I had turned a corner but still had a long way to go as I endured the fight with meningitis for a further six months before I finally recovered.

Not long after my recovery, I got chicken pox. It was awful, I scratched my skin raw and had to be isolated. I also got malaria which meant I had a very high temperature. I lost my appetite and again, suffered from diarrhoea. Despite the forty-degree temperatures outside, I shivered and had cold sweats. Panadol was the only medication that was available but as I am allergic to penicillin, I was unable to take it.

In 1997, I was bitten by a stray dog that was believed to have rabies. I was taken back to the Atapara hospital again, this time to receive the rabies vaccination. When we got to the hospital, they didn't have the vaccination I needed. My parents had some friends who lived nearby and we went to stay there overnight with the plan to try a different hospital the next morning. The dog had bitten me on my leg; it was very painful. My parent's friends cooked fish for dinner that night and as they ate, I played on the floor. I was barefoot and to make matters worse, I stood on a fishbone which became embedded in my foot and the wound later became infected. Not only did I have to recover from a dog bite on one leg, but an infection in the opposite foot. It felt like something that could only happen to me.

I was so skinny as a young girl, that the wind could almost carry me away. But through all my illnesses, I had such amazing support from both my immediate family, and wider family. They would all gather around me, bringing me sweets and killing animals. They would speak to me in the language of my tribe Langi which is Luo. It is a language spoken in Kenya.

In addition to the many challenges my parents and I faced, as a result of my illnesses, war still raged on around us. The Lord's Resistance Army was now a part of everyday life in Northern Uganda.

Up until the time I was eight, I was home schooled by my father who is a teacher. He worked at a government school where he had to teach all the subjects including maths and English. He was teaching English but had only just learned it himself.

Due to the situation with the war, I didn't start school until I was eight years old. I attended Minakulu Primary school where my father taught. He used to beat me at school, but I learned how to protect myself and used to pad my clothes so that the beatings wouldn't hurt. I wouldn't feel a thing. It worked for a while until he became aware of what I was doing and used to slap me on the hand instead.

For me, school was a struggle. For all the children growing up along with me, unless their parents could afford to send them away from the war zone, they simply could not focus on school in the way that children should be able to do. Constantly living in fear meant study could not be a priority. My school was not the place of safety and sanctuary that a school should be. Instead, it was a place of fear.

I remember on one occasion I didn't feel well and told my mother I didn't want to go to school. She thought I was pretending but I begged and pleaded with her. I really wasn't lying and ultimately, she allowed me to stay home.

It was that day that many of my fellow classmates went to school and never came home again. My school was attacked and bombed by the rebels with many children either killed or abducted. It was by the grace of God that my mum was able to see that I really was sick.

The attack happened around mid-day, all the students were all in one class. The entire building was ambushed. Many of my neighbour's children were taken. They'd take children from the age of five and train them to be child soldiers. Those abducting the students were just children themselves. There were children killing children. The girls that were taken were automatically used as sex slaves. Once they were menstruating, they were considered fit for this fate.

As soon as word reached us that the school had been attacked, my mum took me, and my siblings and we had to run as the rebels were on the way to attack the houses in the village.

To this day, there's a wall in that classroom that has never been rebuilt and there's a list of all the students and teachers who either died or went missing on that day, never to return. There is a memorial there every year in their honour.

There was one boy in the village who was taken on another occasion. Eight years later, he returned to the village. He was fourteen at the time but everyone in the village was afraid of him because of what he had been trained to do. He had been told when he was captured by the rebels that his fingers would be chopped off if he didn't do as he was told. If he tried to escape, they told him they would find his family and kill them in front of him. That boy's family gave him some land outside the village, and he stayed there but was never able to integrate back into life in the village due to the horrific combination of what had been done to him and the fear that everyone in the village felt because of what he had done to others. However, due to Government intervention in helping the victims of that war, the boy, who is now a man, has gone on to help others who suffered the same fate as he.

I heard many stories, each one worse than the previous. One girl who was taken was married off to one of the leaders of the Resistance Army and mothered fifteen children. She too has gone on to help others. The war continued from 1986 to 2012 – the victims are countless.

4

We kept running until, as I had learned, the gunfire was silenced, and it was safe to slow down. In the end, we didn't get to my grandmother's house instead stopping in a stranger's home where we had to wait for five days. All that time, the army and rebels continued to fight it out. We hear bombs drop and the gunfire would pick up again. Word would reach us that people we knew had been killed. Finally, on the fifth day, we heard on the radio that the fighting had ended, and we could return to the village.

At the age of six I had learned that running was a matter of survival and by focusing on that, I was able to block out all the other dangers that threatened as I ran barefoot – the poisonous snakes that lurked in the tall grass, the lions and other wild animals that were every bit as deadly as the rebels.

There was an army barracks near our home. The army had been deployed there to protect the civilians from rebel attacks. When the rebels did attack, it was always the army barracks that they would attack first. Hearing the attack, we would know we had no choice but to run. We would be able to see the gunfire in the dark, as the rebels attacked the barracks and the army fought them off, in a bid to buy us more time to escape.

Being close to that barracks helped me in some ways. I used to go there and watch the soldiers to see what they were doing. I would copy the exercises they did, and it meant I was fast and strong on my feet – attributes that certainly saved my life during all those times of running.

This constant living on the edge and in fear meant all us children developed a sharpness. We had no choice but to be constantly alert and ready to flee, being any other way could only bring you closer to abduction or death.

On one occasion, I became separated from my mum and ended up in a field full of people who I didn't know. All that was left to do was sit there and wait until my mother found me.

Another time, when I was about eight, I had gone to the market for my mother. I was a curious child and loved listening to other people's conversations. In the market that day, I heard some people saying that the neighbouring village had been attacked by rebels. That meant that there was every probability our village would be next. I went home and told my mother what I had heard and that we needed to pack our things and leave our home. My father was away at the time at school and my mother raised her eyes to heaven and slapping me on the head told me to stop gossiping and get on with my work.

I stopped talking about what I had heard but I wasn't able to put it out of my mind. I took out a bag and packed my belongings into it before going to bed. In the early hours of the morning, a bomb went off in the market, tearing the whole area apart. Thankfully, those who lived close-by had already fled. Our house was twenty minutes from the market. I was lying on the ground, but I hadn't fallen asleep. I heard the bomb, and I could hear footsteps on the ground outside our house. I jumped up and we fled and ran until we got to our grandmother's house. We stayed there for two weeks that time.

The time spent waiting to return home was the stuff of nightmares. Often, we would be outdoors with no access to shelter, food or water. For days on end, we would just have to sit and wait until it was safe to return home. As a child, I never thought about what any of this meant, I just knew I was hungry or thirsty, extremely cold or dangerously hot. Now, as an adult, I can only imagine what my parents and the other adults were going through during those times of waiting. Stuck in the wilderness without the ability to feed themselves or their children and all that time available to them, filled with thoughts of what they might face as soon as they could return home.

Each and every time we returned; we were greeted with the same devastation. Sometimes our house would be burned to the ground but sometimes not. All our belongings would be gone, and worse, our livestock taken and our crops pillaged.

5

I was eight at the time that my aunt, as I called her, made contact. She had learnt that my father was caring for her mother who was sick at the time. To ease the burden on my father, she asked if he would like for one of his children to go live with her. She offered to help in the upbringing of the child and contribute to education fees. As I was the oldest child in the family, I was the one who was chosen to leave all that was familiar to me, good and bad, and travel to the other side of the world.

It was a monumentally difficult decision for my parents to make. My father was just 5-years old when his cousin left Uganda and so did not remember her. She had never returned to our home country and so my father had had no relationship with her as an adult. She was for all intents and purposes, a stranger to him. On one hand, it would remove me from the warzone that we inhabited and the consistent danger and fear that came with living there. On the other hand, I was their little girl. I had never been anywhere without them and the few times I had left our village was to go to the hospital or to my grandmother's house.

They weighed up the pros and cons. The Lord's Resistance Army was still a terrifyingly significant part of life where we lived. Children continued to be abducted, turned into child soldiers and sex slaves, raped and killed.

My aunt had no family of her own and was in a position to provide me with what seemed like a dream lifestyle in Germany. I could never have had access to in Uganda. She had tried to have children of her own but had not been successful and wanted a blood-relative close to her in her new life. Somebody to whom she could relate. What's more, to my parents, she was offering a life of security, free of danger and fear. They thought about and prayed about it and in the end felt it was what was meant to be.

The decision was made, and preparations got underway for my journey to Germany at the end of 1996. I had no passport and no idea what was happening. I was told I was going to be travelling to the capital to have a photograph taken. Although I wasn't sure of what it all meant, I knew something exciting was happening and so I embraced it. Perhaps it was due to what I had witnessed in the war, but I had come to have no fear. Being afraid to go somewhere would never have occurred to me. Instead, my attitude was *bring it on*!

I was the cause of huge envy in the village. Neighbours were unhappy that I was getting out by going to the city, never mind travelling abroad. There was a mindset in the village that leaving was stepping into an unknown ocean.

In March 1997, I was finally granted a 90-day visa and two days later, saying goodbye to all that was familiar, I was taken to Entebbe airport where I was to take my flight to Munich.

I had never seen a plane in my entire life and the sight of the huge jets was exhilarating. Back then, the air hostesses would look after anyone on the plane who was underage. My dad and some of my uncles came to the airport to see me off. My dad handed me over to an air hostess. He later told me he was mesmerized that I walked away from him with no fear. I turned around just once to wave and smile at him. It affected my father far more than it did me and he recalls a sense of foreboding after he watched the plane take off, that he had done something wrong and made the wrong decision. He regretted his decision the moment I walked away from him but later told me of how proud he was in the strength and confidence that I showed when I walked away from him to travel half way across the world and live with someone I had never met before.

Once airborne, I felt a little sick as the pilot weaved through the sky trying to balance the plane. I was surrounded by strangers and not all of them looked like me – many were white, and I wanted to go touch their skin. I was looked after really well on that flight. The air hostesses would show me pictures of the food that was available, and I'd point to what I wanted.

Landing in Germany, I was processed through all the

various security checks. I had never met my aunt, but I did have a photograph of her. I walked out towards departures where a dog came rushing towards me, wagging its tail. Given my experience of being bitten by a dog in Uganda, the dog terrified me, and I tried to run away from it. I was sure he was going to bite me and not knowing what to do, I stopped and turning around, I kicked the dog.

It was not the best start to my new life, particularly when it transpired that the dog was Appollo who was owned by my aunt. She came running over and swept the dog up in her arms to comfort him. Appollo and I did become friends eventually, but it took some time.

My aunt greeted me and brought me to where she lived. She'd organized a welcome party for me which was quite overwhelming as I didn't speak the language and did not know any of the people. From the start, my aunt referred to me as her daughter and that is how she saw me.

Back in Uganda, my father had gone to stay with his friend as soon as he returned from the airport, the only person he knew who had a phone. He waited there with that man, until my aunt phoned him to confirm that I had arrived safely in Germany. Both my mother and father were hugely relieved that I had completed my journey and began to feel better about their decision to let me go.

Many of my aunt's friends were from different parts of Africa and I got to meet all of them and their children. My aunt was an artist and she brought me to many wonderful places. She brought me to museums and sightseeing. She also brought me shopping. Connecting with other children proved to be difficult. The things they talked about were alien to me, clothes and how our bodies looked, held no interest for me, not after the brutality of all that I had seen. I suspect the circumstances I had lived through had caused me to mature far more quickly than other children of my age.

One of the most notable things about Germany in those early days was the intense cold. I had left the Sahara and arrived at the tail end of a German winter. It was then I saw snow for the first time. It was up to my knees and to make me warm, my aunt had brought me a massive coat and warm boots.

I also had to start school which came as a shock. It was not a good experience as the teachers taught in Dutch, a language I had never heard before. Even my performance in maths, which had been my best subject at home, was not good due to the language barrier. I had a language tutor assigned to me which did help a little.

That was not the most difficult aspect of attending school, however. In the entire school, I was one of only about five black students. As a child, I really didn't see that skin colour could make such a difference in how people would treat me, but I soon learned. The racism became immediately apparent. Not from the teachers but from the students and their parents. None of the other children wanted to play with me or sit with me at lunchtime. The teachers did pair me with another black student, so I did have someone to sit with.

At one school event, one of the students spat at me. Not one to accept such behaviour I took the situation into my own hands, and I beat her. My aunt was called in and other students said what had happened, that the girl had started the altercation. In the end, we both had to stay at home for some time but when we got back to school, the girl came and apologised to me. She was known to be a bully but as I put her in her place, I did not have to deal with any hassle from her again. I knew from an early age that standing up for myself was important.

During my time in Germany, I felt safe from the terror of living in a warzone but that did not stop the constant worry about my parents and the rest of the family. Although I wasn't sure what the feeling was, as an adult I now know that I carried a high level of anxiety with me at all times. It was fear that my parents were in danger or even that they had already died. Any news of attacks by rebels that came to me via the news in Germany made that anxiety worse. A slight respite would come when I got letters from my parents but the time lapse in writing and receiving letters made that respite all too brief.

I slept with pictures of my family and cried myself to sleep every night as I looked at those images. I missed them with a yearning that caused a physical pain. Often, I would be overcome with sadness, but I managed to hide that from people. That sadness caused me to become quiet and I would retreat into myself. I would think about my family all the time, wondering what might be happening to them. Even though I was safe I still carried a huge emotional burden with me.

I didn't have the ability to speak about all that I had seen in Uganda, I kept it all bottled up inside of me. My aunt didn't seem to understand what was going on in my mind. We tried to get used to each other, but it was difficult. She expected me to do a lot of chores around the house, as if I owed her for taking me away from my family and my home. I had been brought up to respect my elders and so, I couldn't express to my aunt, or even to my parents, when I wasn't happy about something. I think my aunt thought I was being difficult and rebellious, and she would get angry with me and hit me. She would talk to me about how difficult my life had been before she rescued me and how ungrateful I was for wanting to lock myself in a bedroom when she had given me this amazing chance for a new life. Wanting to be in my room alone was nothing to do with my aunt, it was just that I wanted to be alone and have the time to process all that had happened and was happening to me.

Conflict with my aunt made me miss my parents even more although I would never dare tell them what was going on. My aunt would communicate with my parents and tell them I was being difficult and not appreciative for all she had done for me. This made my parents angry.

Now I can see what a missed opportunity it was that my aunt was not able to empathise with what I was going through. Perhaps if she had, we could have bonded more closely. She too had fled Uganda due to a brutal regime. When she settled in Europe, she met a German man and got married. During that time, she brought her mother over from Uganda, but she didn't approve of my aunt's new husband. By then my aunt was pregnant but during a fight, her mother punched her in the stomach, and she lost the baby. The injuries she sustained meant her womb had to be removed meaning she would never be able to have the family she so craved.

My aunt would stay up late into the night, talking to me about the terrible things that had happened to her. I knew she had a lot of issues to deal with. We were both grieving in our own way.

My initial visa was for three months but my aunt had it extended for six months. She also went about trying to get me a more permanent visa. That was denied and at the end of 1997, I had to leave Germany and return to Uganda. On the one hand, I knew this meant returning to that constant fear for my life but on the other, I would be returning to the embrace of my family and all that was familiar to me. When I got home my parents questioned me as to why I had been misbehaving. I told them I was sorry and that I had tried to be good. Despite this, I was happy to be home.

6

fell asleep on the first night with my passport around my neck and tucked inside my top. At midnight, I awoke to find my mother shaking me and we fled the house in a bid to escape. This time, the soldiers from the nearby barracks were running alongside. As I ran, one of the soldiers who was running alongside me was struck by a bullet. He fell down dead beside me.

I remember being overwhelmed with exhaustion. Eventually, we came to a house and stopped there. There was a man in the house, and he told everyone they needed to leave as it was no longer safe. My mum and I left, but not everybody did. We headed uphill towards the mountain but about ten people stayed. The man picked me up and carried me. He brought me so far, and then placed me on the ground and said he was going back to see if he could rescue anyone else. From my vantage point where he had carried me, I could see the house as it was whipped into a frenzy of flames. The rebels had set it alight and all of those who remained were killed. If we had waited for just ten more minutes and not done what the man told us to do, my mother and I would certainly have been amongst the dead.

I never saw the man again and I asked other people, but no one knew who I was talking about. Nobody remembered a man telling them to leave.

After the man left, I had to cross a river where the water was up to my chin. The riverbed was thick with plants and foliage, which dragged me down and caused my feet to get caught. At the time, I didn't feel the pain, it was only in the light of the next day when I looked at my legs, I was able to see the cuts and scratches and the dried blood caked in to where I had been cut.

Finally, reaching a field, we joined about sixty-five other people, adults and children who were all sitting and waiting. Three weeks passed and the only access to food we had was what was dropped by Government helicopters. It was a tough reintroduction to life in Uganda following my return from Germany. By now, I had lost the fear of death. I think if someone had pointed a gun at me, I would have shrugged my shoulders. The consistent presence of death and destruction eventually caused it to cease being the horror that it is.

This time when we got home our house had been burned. I was lucky that I had taken my passport with me. It was now clear to me that it was the most valuable thing I owned. Everything that I had brought back with me from Germany was burned. My dad had been away at school when this happened and he came home to see if we were okay but when we got there, my mother and I were gone. There was no way to contact him and so he had to live for days not knowing if we were dead or alive before we were reunited.

In 1998, my aunt managed to get me another 90-day visa and I went back to Germany. But again, she was not successful in getting the visa extended and I had to return once the three months were up.

On leaving Germany, my aunt had agreed with my parents that she would pay for me to attend boarding school on my return home. I was sent to a school far from my home where my native language was not spoken so I was back in an alien education environment until I could grasp another new language.

I still returned to stay with my family during my school holidays and in 1999, our village was attacked at Christmas. We were forced to flee our home yet again and this time we stayed away for a very long time as it was simply not safe to go back. We went all the way to the Sudanese border and waited in a field where the heat was unbearable. Although I didn't know it at the time, that was the last time I went on the run.

From 1998 to 2000 I attended boarding school. It was a challenging experience that I neither loved nor hated. I was away from my family again and the constant fear for their safety remained. It seems that the vast majority of childhood was to be spent alone or amongst strangers.

In this school, my parents paid for someone to look after

me which definitely gave me protection and took away any fears for my own safety. Some of the other children gave me the nickname American Girl, which I hated. I was singled out because I had travelled abroad. I made it work for me in the end and went with it, telling the other students all about my travels and what I'd seen in Germany. I was a good student and my teachers treated me well.

Our school took part in an annual national competition where the students would participate in all aspects of Ugandan culture including sports and dance. I loved to dance and practised hard at my school, for a traditional dance showcasing the struggle of our ancestors. We danced to music that would have been played by our ancestors too. Dancing was a huge part of my time at school.

In 1999, I had been practising for one year for the dance competition but just before we were due to leave to attend the event, my dance teacher told me I hadn't been chosen to participate. I was devastated and so upset about not being chosen. All my family was due to travel from home to attend and I had no way to get word to them that I wouldn't be there to perform. I was eleven at the time, and my friend was chosen to take part which also upset me. I was annoyed with her but eventually got past it and wished her well in the competition.

All the students who were taking part gathered outside the school at 4am to get a bus to where the competition was taking place. At 12 noon the next day, I turned on my radio and I heard that two coaches my schoolmates were travelling on had been involved in a major accident and fifty students, including my friend perished on that day.

When my parents heard what had happened, they immediately thought that I had been in the accident. They rushed to the sight of the crash and were horrified with what they saw. When my parents finally realised that I hadn't been involved, they came to my school. I went to the hospital and saw the dead bodies of my friends, and those who had survived with limbs amputated and other horrific injuries. It was shocking and I realised what a close brush with death I had had. For whatever reason, my teacher did not choose me on that day to take part in the dance competition. Had he made a different decision, it is almost a certainty that I would not have lived beyond that day. It was only later in my life, when I looked back and saw the many dangerous situations I had survived – for reasons unknown it seemed as if my life was being saved. I like to think it was for something better.

After that accident, the school was changed completely. There were only about ten students who remained. It was an eery place and felt unsettling. For a few months after the accident, I continued my education there even though it was as if both my parents and I knew there was something else coming. Having so narrowly escaped the accident and certain death, it now felt as though something good must be just around the corner.

7

N ow, however, she'd had a change of heart and thought that perhaps as some time had passed and I had been given the chance to mature, things might be different. My immediate reaction was that I did not want to go but after giving it some thought, I began to feel that perhaps my destiny was to go abroad and that I should go along with what my aunt was proposing.

The process then had to begin of getting me my visa which was to be far more complicated than acquiring a visa for Germany. We had to travel to Kampala to get a visa which was 600 kilometres away and we made that arduous journey numerous times as we failed over and over to secure my visa.

1999 came to an end and still no visa. I was going back to school while we waited to go try for the visa again. We went in February and again in March but with no success. In April, my aunt urged us to try again. It was the end of the month, and my dad came and got me from school late one evening. I expected that he would take me home to see my mum and my younger siblings, but he didn't. We went by car for part of the journey, and we exited the car at about 11pm that night, when it had taken us as far as it was going to. We waited there for some time, on the side of the road and finally a massive truck came along with some soldiers in it, and they offered to bring us with them, towards Kampala. It was now 1am and at 5am we were stopped at a junction and my dad was fast asleep. I woke him up as I knew something was happening. The truck was surrounded by men with guns and at first, I thought it was night security, but I soon realise the men were robbing the truck.

The robbers said they would kill the driver if they didn't get money. They came down towards us at the back of the truck, carrying AK47s. I begged them not to shoot my dad. The man accompanying the driver was not cooperating and they shot him in the leg. They took all the money my dad had. Luckily, I had hidden my passport on a string around my neck and they didn't see it. If they had, they would surely have taken it.

Eventually, they went away, and we had to wait while the injured man was brought to the hospital. We heard later he survived. Once the man was taken to the hospital, the driver continued towards Kampala, and we finally reached it but were too late to make our appointment for my visa.

We joined the queue early on the next morning. That is how we spent every day, from Monday to Friday, for the next two weeks. Joining the queue early in the morning but never getting to the top of it before the cut-off time of 2pm.

It was the same every day and we were exhausted. The last day was a Friday and before we joined the queue that morning, I told my dad that if we didn't make it that it was a sign and we needed to forget about it.

As 2pm approached, there were three people ahead of us. It was the closest we had come to getting to the top but before we got there the man at the top drew the barricade across and said they were not taking any more people and to come back on Monday.

I looked at my dad and reminded him of what I had said to him earlier. He had spent so much money trying to get me out of Uganda. Money that he could ill-afford and I couldn't stand by and allow him to spend more of his money and his time in a queue that was going nowhere for me.

Without explanation, the man who had pulled across the barricade and told everyone to come back on Monday, looked at me and my dad and beckoned us past the three people ahead of us, to the top of the queue. I had no idea why he singled us out, but he did. Perhaps it was because he had seen us queuing unsuccessfully for so many days. He brought us to be interviewed and he asked who I would meet in the UK. I told him, my aunty, and he asked me about having travelled to Germany before. That was it. He didn't say another word but simply stamped by passport with a six-month visa. Relief flooded over me.

We got word to my aunt, and she booked my ticket for May 20th. It was just a few days away and I would not get home to see my mother or my siblings. It was a more emotional departure than when I had left to go to Germany. At that time, my mum and my siblings, were on the run from rebels and so I feared for their safety. More than that, something told me that I would not see my parents or family again for a very long time.

When I finally got to the UK, I was detained at border control for hours and the authorities thought I was being trafficked. An interpreter had to be called in and my aunt was brought in to ensure our stories corroborated. Eventually, they released me, and I was reunited with my aunty who I hugged with relief.

My school would not be open to me until September, so I enjoyed a great summer with my aunt, going to tourist sites like museums and Buckingham Palace. When I was in Germany, my aunt had many friends but not many of them were black. Now, however, she had befriended a woman who lived next door and had teenagers that were my age and a daughter that was twenty. I could tell immediately that this family had become very close to my aunt and although I can't say that I disliked them, there was something not quite right about the mother.

My aunt also had her boyfriend who at first appeared to be a nice guy and he and I got along well together. My aunt's boyfriend was younger than her and I soon noticed that the woman from next door would bring her daughter a lot to be around my aunt's boyfriend. He was a very attractive man, and something didn't seem right. I said it to my aunty, that she should be careful.

The woman disliked me from the start and warned my aunt to be careful of me and that although my aunt referred to me as 'daughter', I wasn't really her daughter. I was still only twelve at this time and the woman was warning my aunt that I might become intimate with her boyfriend. She was hugely envious of my aunt and was annoyed when my aunt had anything that she didn't.

Ultimately, this woman, for reasons unknown, began to collude with my aunt's boyfriend in trying to get my aunt to send me home. He was from Togo and had not yet received his legal immigration status. He felt that I had the potential to supplant him in my aunt's affections and so, he was only too happy to go ahead with the neighbour's devious plans. Together, they made my life a misery.

My aunt's fiancé would accuse me of stealing which would make me feel terribly upset. Once that behaviour started, I stopped trusting him and I would become very quiet. He would then accuse me of not liking him and my aunt would ask me why I didn't like him. It wasn't that I didn't like him it was because I was afraid of what else he might accuse me of.

Once, my aunt came close to sending me back home because he told her I had taken money from him. She called my dad and told him she was booking my ticket back home. Her fiancé was delighted, his face was lit up with happiness.

He claimed five hundred pounds had gone missing. My aunt flogged me as punishment and banished me to my room. I took myself upstairs and locked myself in my room. I had decided to wait it out until it was time to go back home. Just before I was due to leave to go back home, the money was found. My aunt's fiancé did apologise but it marked the end of any chance we had of being able to establish a decent relationship.

My aunt soon got back to her old ways and would stay up late at night, smoking and drinking and keeping me awake so that she had someone to talk to about her past. That happened every night, even if I was asleep, she would wake me up to talk.

When I did start school, I used to have to walk to the bus. The neighbour's children would throw eggs at me, and laugh at me and call me burnt, due to my dark colour. I had developed a toughness after all I'd been through and I made it clear to them their words didn't bother me but if they touched me physically, I'd fight back.

One day, a gang of them cornered me and beat me very badly. I had to stay home from school for two weeks to recover. What was worse, was that my aunt didn't believe me despite all my teachers telling her that I was a good student and not a troublemaker.

To distract myself from the misery they caused me, I found myself in the library where I asked the librarian to help me with my English. She was a kind woman and obliged. From then on, every day after school and during my holidays, I put all my efforts into learning English.

At school I hated English literature as we were studying Romeo and Juliet. The teacher would make me read aloud and all the students would laugh at my accent and pronunciation. It was that summer that I really went full throttle with my English studies with the help from my lovely librarian friend. Once back in class in September, the English teacher asked us to write about what we'd done during the summer. I was able to write a fantastic composition for which I was awarded an A-plus. My teacher was flabbergasted.

My best friend in that school was from Senegal. We didn't speak each other's languages and she didn't speak good English. I don't know how we communicated but we fast became partners in crime. Later, the librarian also helped me learn how to use a computer. She became a close friend and was instrumental in helping me get ahead in what were tough days.

School in the UK was definitely easier than in Germany. There was much more multiculturalism and so I didn't stand out like I had in Munich. We all spoke our native languages and communicated with each other in English. I did encounter bullying at the very beginning. There was one mean girl, as there always is. She made herself known when I sat in her seat in the dining hall. I had no idea it was her seat, and the girl came over to me when I was eating my lunch and threw it on the floor. I stood up and grabbed her and beat her. It caused some problems, and I was given a disciplinary letter to give to my aunt. It turned out to be a blessing as she never bothered me again.

I did well in sports and so everyone wanted me for their team. I belonged to the afterschool club and became involved in drama. Some friends and I formed a girl band too.

The year 2001 quickly started on a downward spiral. My aunt's fiancé became ill and was admitted to hospital. Three months after that, my aunt was also admitted to hospital due to mental illness.

There was a period when I was left to look after myself. In addition to that, I was the only person my aunt recognised. After school every evening, I would travel 30 minutes to visit my aunt and bring her food, as she wouldn't eat the hospital food. I wasn't entirely alone in our house as my aunt had one of the rooms rented out but still, the person who rented the room was not someone that I knew and was out at work all day. I was just 13 years old.

My aunt recognized me, but we couldn't have a normal conversation. Eventually, her fiancé was released from hospital and by July my aunt had returned to normal, and she was allowed to come home too. Soon after that, preparations for the wedding got underway and they were married.

During this time, the woman next door became increasingly difficult. She would throw her rubbish from her garden into ours. They'd throw eggs and flour at the house and dirt at our windows. They would stand and laugh at me as I cleaned it up. It was horrible. No matter what my aunt had, the woman could not be happy for her. Latterly, my aunt saw what the woman was really like and stopped talking to her.

8

2001 had started badly but got progressively worse. Towards the end of the year, my aunt got a phone call from her bank manager to say that her bank account had been emptied. There was nothing left in it. She was in shock and had no idea what he was talking about. She questioned and questioned but could not find any answers. Both the money in her current account and her savings account was gone.

She had recently bought a new car and received an updated bank statement confirming what was in her account but in just a short period, all that money vanished into thin air. My aunt believed that her neighbour was somehow responsible, but she was never able to prove it. The neighbour had threatened us on many occasions and said she would ensure we would be left with nothing. Although there was no proof that she was involved, her threats came to life.

When there was no money to pay the rent, the landlord who was very kind, allowed us to stay for two months. But after that we had to leave. All the time I had known my aunt, she had helped so many people but now when she was in need, so many people turned their backs on her.

We had nowhere to go. My aunt's husband, as he now was, had a cousin who lived in a council flat in a high rise building in Birmingham. It was in one of the worst places in the city and was very unsafe. It was called Lozells, and was so dangerous, it felt like being back in the war in Uganda. There were drug dealers everywhere and gunshots would be heard frequently throughout the day. It was known for gang culture and for prostitution. If I was going out of our flat and the lift was broken, which it often was, I'd have to climb down flights of stairs and endure all these men making remarks about my appearance. It was terrifying. While I lived there an 18-year-old woman was pushed down the stairs and killed. There was constant music and noise, the smell of weed and a general feeling of depravation and unease.

The situation between my aunt and her husband began to deteriorate at that time. She suffered from diabetes and when we moved to Birmingham first, she got a job in a care home. I used to go with her and spend time with the patients in the home, mostly to escape how terrible life in the flat was. After some time though, she had to quit her job as her diabetes was causing problems with her legs. Her husband became emotionally abusive, accusing her of being lazy and demanding that she go out and get a job, but she simply wasn't able.

All the while I was living through these circumstances, the war continued in Uganda and my family continued to live in tremendous danger. My dad decided at that time, he'd had enough of running and simply wasn't going to do it again. My family had dug an underground tunnel behind our house. It was a contingency. Somewhere to hide if the rebels attacked and we didn't have enough time to leave the house.

The rebels did attack one day when my father was home alone and instead of running, he went out the back and got into the tunnel. He could hear the rebels searching close by as he covered himself and hunkered down. He could hear our animals howling as the rebels untied them and took them away. As they came closer, he could feel them and see their guns. They searched and searched but thankfully they didn't find him.

Meanwhile, as I carried the worry of all that was happening at home, my life in the UK continued at an absolute low point. We had no money, and occasionally when I did get money, I would save it so that at times when there was no food, I would have a backup plan to feed myself. I spent most of my days cleaning the flat. There was no washing machine, so I hand washed everyone's clothes. The expectation was that I was staying there for free, so I had to pay for my keep. I cooked, cleaned and washed clothes for me, my aunt, her husband and her husband's cousin. Basically, I became a domestic slave. I remember gazing out the window and wondering if this was going to be the rest of my life. I worried constantly about my family back home and if they were safe. There was even less opportunity to contact them than there had been when we were in London.

An inner dialogue played on repeat in my mind telling me there was more than this, something good had to happen, there was something better out there for me. After all that had happened to me, from running for my life in Uganda, to escaping death, travelling half-way across the world and adjusting to an alien country where I didn't speak the language – I had met the challenges of it all head on. My inner voice spoke to me and clearly said, 'I am Christine and I know I am meant for more than this.'

Thank you for purchasing this book.

If you want to learn and find out what Christine Glory is up to, you can connect with her in the following ways:

Email: christineglory.mentor@gmail.com
Facebook: https://www.facebook.com/Christineglory.mentor/
Instagram: www.instagram.com/Christine.Glory
Website: https://linktr.ee/christine.glory

Thank you for your support

Story Terrace

9 781739 667818